George Perkins Clinton

**Broom-corn smut**

George Perkins Clinton

**Broom-corn smut**

ISBN/EAN: 9783337141301

Printed in Europe, USA, Canada, Australia, Japan

Cover: Foto ©Andreas Hilbeck / pixelio.de

More available books at **www.hansebooks.com**

# UNIVERSITY OF ILLINOIS,

# Agricultural Experiment Station.

## URBANA, MARCH, 1897.

## BULLETIN No. 47.

## *BROOM-CORN SMUT.

### RELATIONSHIP.

*Related plants.* Broom-corn is placed by botanists in the genus Andropogon (Sorghum), one of the prominent genera of the grass family. Closely related to this plant are a number of other cultivated forms commonly known as sorghum, durra, Kafir corn, Jerusalem corn, etc. These are considered by Hackel as descended from a common ancestor and are therefore placed by him as varieties under the species *Andropogon Sorghum,* of which broom-corn is designated as *Andropogon Sorghum* var. *technicus.* In different parts of the world, usually in the warmer regions, certain of these varieties have assumed considerable importance; especially during the last few years all of them have been more largely cultivated in the United States and seem to merit this increased attention. Any fungus or insect found at work on them, therefore, may be considered of direct economic importance, especially when serious injury is inflicted.

*Related smuts.* It is the purpose of this article to discuss at length one of the fungous troubles of this group of plants—a fungus that is commonly designated as smut. As there are several species that have been found on one or another of these plants, it may be well to consider briefly all of the smuts before proceeding to the

*For those who may wish merely to get from this bulletin the practical method of preventing broom-corn smut, there has been prepared at the end, under " Prevention of broom-corn smut," directions for the use of hot water in the treatment of broom-corn seed. Also under "Summary," immediately preceding the above, are given briefly some of the chief points that the bulletin presents. The writer wishes to acknowledge indebtedness and return thanks to the several botanists and to the growers and dealers in broom-corn who have conferred such favors as the loan of specimens, references to literature, information concerning the injury and loss caused by the smut, etc. 373

discussion of this particular one. From Cairo, Egypt, there has been reported a smut in the flower parts of a variety of Andropogon grown there. In this the spores adhere in small round balls, and so the fungus is placed in the genus Sorosporium (*Sorosporium Ehrenbergii*), although originally the specimen was incorrectly referred to a species of Ustilago (*Ustilago Reiliana* *). So far it seems to have been collected from that locality only. On the same plant from central Asia another smut has been reported, which by its discoverer, Sorokine, was described as a type of a new genus, Endothlaspis; but later it has been placed by De-Toni doubtfully in the genus Cintractia (*Cintractia Sorghi*). Tracy and Earle report a single specimen of this from Mississippi, collected in 1888. An examination of this specimen, however, shows that its spores are larger than those of *Cintractia Sorghi*, as described by De-Toni, and it corresponds so closely with *Ustilago Reiliana* that it seems proper to consider it as belonging to that species. There are three smuts apparently of the Ustilago type that have been found on one or another of these varieties. The most conspicuous is head smut (*Ustilago Reiliana*), which turns the whole panicle into a smutty mass. This is more common than the above, being reported from Africa, Europe, and from two or three places in the United States. The second one (*Ustilago cruenta*) occurs in less conspicuous outbreaks on the rays of the panicle, occasionally on the stem itself, and in the flower parts. While a common form in certain parts of Europe, this smut has not yet been reported in this country. The third form (*Ustilago Sorghi*) is quite similar to the second but limits its attacks to the young inner flower parts, producing a seed-like body filled with its spores.

*Identity of broom-corn smut.* A comparison of the specimens of smuts collected on the sorghum-like plants in Kansas, Illinois, New Jersey, and Wisconsin with European specimens of the above Ustilagos leads to the conclusion that the smuts so far collected in this country, when limited to the reproductive parts of the flower, belong to the species *Ustilago Sorghi*. In fact this is the species to which they have always been referred. *Ustilago cruenta* and *Ustilago Sorghi*, however, are very closely related. The chief differences between them that can be gathered from an examination of descriptions and specimens are that the former may occur on any part of the panicle or even on the stem, while the latter is confined to the flower; that the former has spores that average larger and are more variable in size and shape than the latter; that the individual spores of the former are more apt to have a reddish tint while the latter usually have a distinct olive tint.

---

* See de Thümen Mycotheca universalis, No. 725.

The reason for doubting the identity of our specimens was caused by the description of the life history[1] of *Ustilago cruenta* as given by Brefeld, especially the germination,[2] which seems to agree very closely with what we have learned concerning the smut on broom-corn, and also by the statement made by him that *Ustilago Sorghi*[3] did not germinate in water, which seems to be a very characteristic thing with the smut with which we have dealt. It is barely possible that the Ustilago with which his chief investigations were carried on might be considered by some botanists as *Ustilago Sorghi*, instead of *Ustilago cruenta*, as they were with a smut that was entirely confined to the inflorescence. But certainly the evidence as a whole justifies the conclusion that our American specimens belong to the species called *Ustilago Sorghi*.

This point in its identity having been settled, another difficulty arose when a study was made of the spore formation of the fungus. This showed that it agreed in this respect with the genus Cintractia rather than with Ustilago, and if we are to regard these as distinct genera, our fungus must be considered as belonging to the former. *Endothlaspis Sorghi* of Sorokine, as has been stated, is now referred by De-Toni questioningly to Cintractia, and what was described originally as a quite distinct smut is really rather closely related to our form. It is not unlikely that an examination of the spore formation of *Ustilago cruenta* would also show something of this character. A careful examination of the type specimens and of collections obtained from the different countries where these smuts have been reported, together with a study of their spore formation and germination, is needed to bring out their true systematic relationships. However, having settled upon the identity of our form as a Cintractia and as the species commonly called *Ustilago Sorghi*, let us next consider its hosts and distribution.

### HOSTS AND DISTRIBUTION.

*In general.* This smut has been reported from a number of the countries of southern Europe, also from Africa, Asia, and the United States; and has for its host several of the different varieties of *Andropogon Sorghum*. It was brought to the United States through imported seed of these plants. Just when and where it first made its appearance it is impossible to state; but from the ease with which it attacks broom-corn it was probably at the place where that plant was first largely grown. The first printed reference that has been found is that made by Trelease, in his "Preliminary List of Parasitic Fungi of Wisconsin," printed in 1884.

---

[1] Untersuchungen aus dem Gesammtgebiete der Mykologie 11: 43–51. [2] Ibid 5: 91–93. [3] Ibid 12: 120.

In this he mentions the finding of the fungus at Madison, and also states that Sturtevant reports it from New York and Farlow from the District of Columbia, in all three cases on plants raised from imported Chinese seed. Professor Farlow in answer to inquiries concerning the Columbia specimen writes that it was sent to him from the Department of Agriculture at Washington and was taken from sorghum grown in New Jersey in 1882. In 1889 Webber reported the finding of the smut on Millo maize in Nebraska, and in 1890 Failyer and Willard found the same on several imported varieties grown for the first time at the Kansas Experiment Station. Professor Hitchcock in answer to a letter gives the following plants upon which it has been collected in Kansas : sorghum (Early Amber, Rangoon, Red Liberian, and many unknown varieties), broom-corn, Kafir corn. Though not reported from Ohio so far as can be learned, it probably has occurred there, as considerable broom-corn has been raised in that state.

*In Illinois.* The first collections made in Illinois that are represented in the herbarium at the University of Illinois were those made by M. B. Waite in August, 1887, at Urbana. In 1888 in the Proceedings of the American Society of Microscopists, Burrill notes the smut as occurring in this state on both broom-corn and sorghum, and this is the first printed reference to the smut here that has been found. No further collections or study was made until the spring of 1894, when John Marten, assistant to the State Entomologist, in studying the insect pests of broom-corn at Arcola, brought specimens to the botanical department with the report that this was considered one of the worst pests of the plant in that vicinity. The study of the fungus in its relation to broom-corn was then undertaken by the botanical department of the Experiment Station, the results of which are given in this bulletin.

### INJURY AND LOSS.

*Effect of attack.* The importance of a fungous disease depends in great part on the place and character of its attack. What is the effect of this fungus upon its host? As with the smuts of wheat and oats, one cannot tell the infected plant from the free until the floral parts are protruded through the upper leaves. Examination then shows that the infected plants have the place of the seed occupied by a usually enlarged body, having on the outside a reddish covering and within a dusty mass of spores. All the seeds of an infected panicle are usually destroyed. The first noticeable injury, then, is the prevention of seed formation.

In the case of broom-corn this loss is not nearly so serious as in the case of those cereals that are raised especially for the seed.

An examination of the brush of an infected plant, unfortunately, shows that it is of a very inferior grade, usually almost worthless. Here, then, is a much more important loss, for the brush is the part for which broom-corn is raised. Good broom-corn has the rays of about uniform thickness and length and all springing from a series of very contracted nodes so as to give them about the same point of origin. In the case of infected plants these internodes are usually elongated, and the rays are of unequal lengths, so that there are a series of irregular rays arranged on an elongated and thickened central axis—qualities very undesirable. Among growers of broom-corn this elongated and thickened axis is not always recognized as the work of the fungus. This is probably due to the fact that occasionally plants apparently free from the fungus show brush of this character. Such are but tendencies to a reversion toward the original type of the plant; and, possibly, even in such cases an imprisoned vegetative state of the fungus cut off from spore formation may at times be the inciting cause. It is a fact, however, that in the many hundreds of smutty panicles examined this tendency to spread out the contracted axis was always more or less manifested. The number of large normal sized rays is also less on such a plant. For instance, in each of two different varieties the principal rays were counted on ten free and ten affected plants selected at random. In every case the number in the free plants exceeded those in the infected, while the average for one was fifty-five on free plants and thirty-three on infected, and for the other was forty-eight on free and thirty-seven on infected plants. The energy in such plants has gone into the elongated axis and not in enlarging all the rays.

Smut may also produce some damage by the spores settling on the brush when this is gathered with moisture on it. These stick to the plant when the moisture evaporates, and although they may in part be shaken off the appearance of the brush is still very apt to be affected. This, however, must not be confused, as it is by some, with the trouble that arises when broom-corn is stored wet or in a damp place. Under such a condition a saprophytic fungus of an entirely different nature is very apt to appear on the plants, causing them to have a deadened color and to become blackish where the fungous threads show. This trouble affects very decidedly the color and strength and consequently the value of the brush. Smut is, finally, a bad thing because of the disagreeable dust that is produced when plants so affected are thrashed

*Abundance.* A second factor that determines the importance of
a fungous disease is its abundance or distribution. What per cent.
of broom-corn plants are infected by smut, and how does this per
cent. vary from year to year? In 1895 Mr. Duncan, of the firm
of Duncan & Tarbox, broom-corn dealers at Arcola, said in re-
sponse to inquiries that broom-corn had been raised in that region
for thirty-five years, and while at first smut was not noticed it had
gradually increased in amount. Mr. B. F. Cox, a dealer at the
same place, also expressed a belief that smut was more abundant
than formerly, and gave as a rough estimate that an average of
one per cent. of the plants were smutty. An examination of a few fields in the vicinity that year showed them usually
with less than one per cent. smutted. One very smutty field,
however, gave in parts of it twenty per cent. The few growers
seen seemed to think that smut was less than usual, though a year
or two previous it had been unusually abundant. In 1896 letters of
inquiry to various buyers and raisers in the vicinity of Arcola and
Tuscola brought the uniform reply that it had been a year in
which broom-corn was quite free from smut.

In our experiments here broom-corn, raised from seed such
as is ordinarily planted, gave in different plats during the two
years yields varying from one to twenty per cent. smutty; while
that raised from very smutty seed gave from ten to fifty per cent.
In 1896 the plants here, unlike those in the broom-corn district,
were unusually smutty. It is generally true that the seed that is
ordinarily planted produces plants in which the amount of smut
varies from practically nothing up to three to five per cent., or,
under exceptionally favorable conditions for the fungus, a still
higher per cent. may be expected; while seed that is very smutty
is always likely to give a crop with considerable smut, the per
cent. of which under conditions favorable to it becomes very large.

*Value of crop.* The importance of a fungous disease depends
lastly upon the value of the host as a commercial plant. In the
United States broom-corn is largely raised in parts of Kansas,
Illinois, and possibly in a few other states. The area devoted to
its culture in 1895 was estimated at over two hundred thousand
acres.[1] Of this area Kansas[2] claimed about one hundred thirty-
five thousand acres, producing a crop valued at over one million
two hundred twenty thousand dollars. The next year, however,
the acreage dropped to less than forty thousand. The secre-
tary[3] of the State Board of Agriculture for Illinois gave the area in
this state for 1895 as over twenty-five thousand acres, a slight

[1] Irrig. Age 9:— Ja. 1896. [2] Rep. St. Bd. Agr. Kans. 15:794. 1896. [3] Statist.
Rep. Ill. St. Bd. Agr. Dec. 1895:5. 1895.

decrease from the preceding year. This Illinois acreage gave a
yield of over eighty-five hundred tons, the value of which, estimated at the average price of the time, was over three hundred
thirty thousand dollars. Broom-corn, while raised in a small way
in a number of different counties, is extensively grown in Coles
and Douglas only, situated in central eastern Illinois. Here it is
one of the principal crops, amounting to three-fourths of all that
is raised in the state.

*Financial loss.* Judging from the above facts can this smut
be counted as an important pest? In other words, is it injurious
enough to merit attempts at prevention? If the seed of broom-
corn was the part for which the plant is raised (its loss when at-
tacked by the smut usually being total and the per cent. of infested plants being easily estimated) the loss in dollars in particular cases or even in general for a district could be fairly estimated, as is done in the case of smutted oats and wheat; but as
the case is an estimate of loss would be largely guess work. No
aim, therefore, is made here to estimate the loss other than to
state that it is often great enough to make preventive measures
desirable. That it is at least serious enough for this seems to be
the uniform opinion of those interested in the culture of the
plant. In order to determine the estimate placed upon the fungus a number of letters were sent to prominent growers of broom-
corn at Arcola and Tuscola, and several of the answers to three
of the questions asked are given here:

1. Is smut one of the prominent enemies of broom-corn, and would it be
of much benefit if it could be prevented?
2. Do you use means to keep broom-corn free from it? What?
3. How does it injure broom-corn?

1. Yes. 2. Plant seed that is not affected with it. 3. By blackening
it after it gets wet before it is thrashed. Most of the heads that have smut on
them are of no account.

Arcola, Ill. W. C. CUPPY.

1. Smut is an enemy of broom-corn, and it would be a decided benefit to
prevent it. 2. The means we use is to select seed that has no smut on it. 3.
You lose the head that has smut on it, and if the cane is damp when you seed
it, it colors the rest and injures the sale.

Tuscola, Ill. A. B. SAWYER.

1. Smut is one of the enemies, and it would be an advantage if prevented.
2. I am careful to use seed that has not been infected with it. 3. If cleaned
when damp or with dew on it darkens the brush.

Arcola, Ill. D. S. HARRIS.

1. Yes. 2. No. 3. It makes it a light or white color and the brush
is brittle and of light weight. I think the time it is planted and the season
has a good deal to do with it, as some years it is worse than others. It was
the worst in 1893, a very dry season after the tenth of June.

Tuscola, Ill. NATHANIEL MOORE.

1. Yes. 2. Yes, by washing in copperas. 3. It makes it bad to handle all the way through, and if it rains while it is on the table in the field it causes it to turn black. I think that it is in the seed that is planted, and the longer seed is planted (that is seed that has smut in it or in the field from which it came) the more smut there will be.

Arcola, Ill.                                    CHARLES WESCH.

1. Yes. In my opinion it would. 2. Only by trying to secure seed free from smut. 3. By blasting, causing large fiber of a coarse, worthless quality. Also when cleaned when damp it adheres to the other heads, turning them black.

Arcola, Ill.                                    F. G. HASTEN.

Let us now turn from the economical consideration of smut and study it in detail as a plant in its various phases of development.

## LIFE HISTORY.

*Nature of smut.* We have been proceeding so far on the assumption that the nature of smut is understood by the reader. It is a fact, however, that all growers of broom-corn do not realize that smut is a plant, though of low development, just as much as is broom-corn, which is one of high development. The vague ideas held by some may be illustrated by the fact that such think smut is the result of insect work, or that it is a "bastard growth due to the effect of sorghum on broom-corn," etc.

Smut belongs to the very low group of plants called fungi— plants of very simple development, usually of very small size, and destitute of the power of directly forming their food out of mineral matter, moisture, and gases. This being the case, fungi must get their food from either dead or living organic matter In the case of smut it gets its food from the living broom-corn plant, and so it is called a parasitic fungus. Like broom-corn it has a vegetative part concerned with obtaining the supply of food and with growth, and a reproductive part concerned chiefly with the production of future individuals like itself. The vegetative part is technically known as mycelium, and is composed of thread-like cells concealed entirely within the tissues of the broom-corn. The reproductive bodies are known as spores, and the multitudes of these minute cells are what constitute the visible portion of the fungus in the "smutted" parts of the host.

*Spores.* The character of the visible outbreaks seem to vary somewhat in the different varieties. This is probably due to the differences in the surrounding tissues or other peculiar characteristics of each host. In general, however, a somewhat elongated and thickened seed-like body is formed. In broom-corn this, compared with the normal seed, is usually a slightly enlarged ovate or oblong formation. A careful examination of these while young shows that they have taken the place of the young pistil and stamens, rarely merely the former while the latter have come to a somewhat normal development. Frequently these parts are infected so early that they have become blended together and the identity of the stamens entirely or nearly lost (pl. 3, fig. 6). In 1895 specimens were found that varied considerably from this normal type. Here the outbreaks were more elongated (half an inch) and with somewhat closely appressed branches. Evidently these represented an infection of the whole flower, or possibly of more than one flower. The specimens were thought at first to be a distinct species, but the appearance and germination of the spores and all gradations between this and the normal form showed the two to be the same (pl. 3, fig. 7 and 8). The difference in appearance was evidently only the result of an earlier and hence more widespread spore formation. In all of these outbreaks there is on the outside a somewhat reddish membrane, while the space within is taken up with a dusty mass of spores, save in the center where there is a distinct, slender and hard mass of tissue, referred to by Winter as the "columella."

Examined under the microscope the individual spores have a brownish color with a distinct olive tint, though in mass to the naked eye they are of a very dark reddish brown color. They are single celled bodies of a sub-spherical shape and from 5 to 8 thousandths of a millimeter in diameter,[1] though varying occasionally from the above in both shape and size. The protoplasmic contents fill the spore and are frequently somewhat granular so as to give the spore wall the appearance of being minutely papillate.

*Germination.* When placed in water these spores germinate readily. No other of the many smuts whose germination in water we have tried has germinated so readily and vigorously as this. It germinates equally well as soon as formed or when a year old. Specimens kept in a dry room germinated whenever placed in water at various intervals during more than three years, though less abundantly and easily the last year. De Bary states that von Liebenberg caused the spores to germinate after being in the herbarium six and a half years.

The general character of the germination depends on the fluid in which the spores are placed. In water, while there was a difference in degree between different spores in the same culture, and, while at different times perhaps all conditions were not exactly the same and so varied the character somewhat, still the gen-

---

[1] This size may be better appreciated by the many readers when it is stated that there are millions of these spores in each of the seed-like bodies.

eral phenomena were as follows: Within six to ten hours after being placed in the water many of the spores show the beginning of germination by the appearance in each case of a minute hyaline papilla, which gradually grows out into a thin-walled tube having a rounded and slightly pointed apex, but showing no constriction where it emerges from the spore. Some spores have shown this stage of germination within three hours after being placed in the water. This germ-tube, or pro-mycelium, elongates until it is three to five times as long as the diameter of the spore, this being accomplished within less than twenty-four hours after germination begins, frequently in about half that time. Two or three cross-partitions are now formed at right-angles to the tube, dividing it into three or four about equal cells. These septa are rather faint at first, and while the tube is filled with protoplasmic contents are not always clearly made out. A slight staining, however, serves to bring them out much clearer. At the end of one or more of these cells a short and usually narrow outgrowth appears which bends over and fuses with the adjoining end of the next cell. Usually this outgrowth is so closely appressed that it appears as if the septum had not been formed clear across the tube on that side (pl. 5, fig. 3). These form the so-called buckle or knee joints, and the tube frequently has more or less of a bend where they occur. In a number of cases these buckle joints were seen to be formed by the union of protuberances extending from each side of the septum. Not infrequently these slender outgrowths are less closely appressed to the tube and make quite a growth before joining the pro-mycelium at some more remote point (pl. 5, fig. 2). From these buckle joints, or the end of the pro-mycelium, frequently a thread, usually much more slender than the main tube, grows out to a varying length, forming what I have called infection-threads, because of their similarity to those produced by the sporidia. If these threads attain any considerable length, they show an irregular curving rather than a growth in a straight line like the pro-mycelium. Sometimes the pro-mycelium also gives rise to a lateral branch near the base of about the same diameter as itself. Sporidia are generally produced, though not always very abundantly. Occasionally one can be seen forming either on the end of the pro-mycelium or at the apex of one of the cells. It appears as a small outgrowth having a very narrow connection with the tube, enlarges gradually and is very easily broken from its connection, so that sporidia are usually only seen free in the water. Usually they did not germinate, neither did they seem to reproduce, yeast-like, after being formed. Frequently a large part of the pro-mycelium is early cut off from the spore by an abstriction near the base. These free bodies are somewhat like sporidia in appearance, but can be told by their larger size and the presence of one or two septa. They go through the same development as if remaining connected with the spore.

The preceding germinations were produced chiefly in distilled water; but when large numbers of spores are placed in the fluid, as was usually the case, possibly a little nutritive material is also introduced. Whether the spores are immersed in an abundance of water or are merely covered with a film so as to admit of contact with the air has also something to do with determining the character of germination. In the latter case the pro-mycelium is more apt to run out into a slender thread which is many times the length of the pro-mycelium and not so sharply marked off from it. The protoplasm is confined to the distal end of this thread, the empty part becoming regularly septate. In some few cases I found that in time these threads even gave rise to sporidia and secondary sporidia. The sporidia and secondary sporidia are also more apt to be formed on and to adhere to the pro-mycelium.

In nutrient solutions the chief differences observed from the preceding were the more luxuriant, though not necessarily more abundant, germination, and the formation of more sporidia. In the cases where a weak nutrient fluid of tomato-broth was used the chief differences were the somewhat larger pro-mycelia, the presence in the fluid of more free sporidia, infection threads of greater diameter and usually of greater length. In beef-broth this luxuriant growth of the pro-mycelium was still greater; the sporidia were formed very abundantly and were not easily detached; and, while connected or when fallen off, formed secondary sporidia by the yeast-like manner of sprouting; the sporidia were also larger, especially in diameter, as were also the branches or infection-threads that were formed. When the beef-broth became weakened sufficiently, the sporidia ceased their sprouting and formed the narrow infection-threads quite similar to those usually produced in water from the pro-mycelium.

*Infection of host.* This apparently takes place through the penetration of the epidermis by the infection-threads of the pro-mycelium as well as by those of the sporidia. Entrance into the plant can occur only when the cells are young, and successful infection only through that part of the plant where the threads can reach the growing tip of the plant before the tissues through which it must pass are very old. Thus the germinating seed in its early stages is the only place where broom-corn is liable to become successfully infected. As a germinating plant becomes older and its tissues harder of penetration by the threads, infection becomes less possible until, at the time when the plant breaks through the ground and its first leaves show, it is practically exempt from successful infection.   Brefeld has shown with *Ustilago cruenta* on a similar host that the germs can enter the very young leaves of even large plants, but can not form the mycelium fast enough to reach the growing tip before it is cut off by the maturing of the tissues.

In germination broom-corn shows a common type among grasses—an epicotyl, or sort of an underground internode, is formed connected at one end with the seed and at the other bearing the leaf-sheath with the enclosed young leaves and growing tips.   The epicotyl usually lengthens enough to bring the leaf-sheath above ground, and about this time the growth of the latter is stopped so that it is soon pierced at its apex by the growing leaves within.   Young plants upon the seed of which spores were placed before germination, after they had produced plants of the above or a little later stage, were frequently examined for mycelium ; when this was found it was most abundant at the juncture of the epicotyl and leaf-sheath, and rarely extended very far down into the epicotyl.   Plants at this age also became infected when the leaf-sheath was removed and spores placed on the young leaves at its base, but did not become infected when the spores were merely placed on the outside of the base of the leaf-sheath.   The direction of the mycelium in all these cases was chiefly toward the center of the plant and up.  As this (region near juncture of epicotyl and leaf-sheath) is the shortest path through the plant tissues to the growing apex, it is the most certain and probably the most common place for successful infection, and the earlier the threads enter the more certain they are to reach the growing tip.   After entering it is quite likely that the threads spread in all directions, if there is no difference in resistance , but the maturing cells gradually limit this until finally only the mycelium that has reached the young growing parts keeps up a vigorous growth.

*Mycelium.*   When once the infection-threads succeed in entering the plant at the proper place and time, their further growth is assured by the nourishment that is taken from the plant, and so they soon become independent of the sporidia or spores to which they are attached on the outside.   They rapidly grow into long, irregularly branched, colorless and thin walled threads that ramify through the tissue of the plant.   The diameter of these threads (2–4 microns) is considerably enlarged from that of the infection-thread, whose very small diameter is more favorable for penetration of the epidermal cells. These threads now constitute the mycelium of the fungus. This is not confined to the intercellular spaces but runs as readily through the cells. It is found most abundantly in patches in the parenchyma cells which in the epicotyl form a band several cells deep surrounding a central cylinder of the wood cells. At the juncture of the leaf-sheath where the central cylinder begins to separate into the distinct bundles, the mycelial threads run into the parenchyma cells surrounding the bundles. They were also found in the base of the leaf-sheath and in the lower parts of the first leaves.

At first the threads are filled with protoplasm, but as they become older this is more or less lost, and septa are found at irregular intervals; frequently the cell walls are swollen or the contents so changed that the lumen of the thread is not distinctly made out. In the older infected parts there is frequently some discoloration of the threads and of the surrounding plant cells, but in parts but newly infested there is no disturbing condition shown. As these threads penetrate further in the plant they become more limited to the intercellular spaces, and the branches that penetrate into the cells for nourishment assume more of a special appearance (pl. 4, fig. 5). Reaching the young pith cells a short distance below the growing point as new cells are formed they gradually become infested and thus the fungus follows the upward growth of the plant during the entire season. After an infected plant has made its full growth, the mycelium can often be found scattered through the pith in the various internodes generally most abundant in the region of the nodes. Thus mycelium has been found in the very base and in the very apex of plants, a distance of eight or ten feet apart. It is very improbable, however, that there is a continuous connection of the mycelium for even any great part of this distance, for according to Brefeld, the lengthening of the internodes tends to destroy the continuity of the threads. It is always only the mycelium in the vicinity of the tip of the plant that is the active growing part of the fungus.

*Spore formation.* Such is the history of the fungus until the time the broom-corn begins to form its flower parts, and all this time the infected plant, so far as appearance goes, is similar to the one that is not infected. The mycelium penetrates the young ovaries and stamens usually before they are very much differentiated. If this penetration is very early, then the stamens and ovary are not differentiated from each other in the smutted body; but if the fungus has been backward in its penetration, then the smutted part shows ovary and stamens more or less grown together but still so that they can easily be made out as these organs;

occasionally the penetration is even so late that the stamens are free from the spores, only the ovary containing them. Flowers of an infected plant were examined that were so young that the stamens and ovary showed only as small undifferentiated outgrowths of cells from the growing point, and while no mycelium was definitely made out in these, still it was found among the young cells in their vicinity, thus indicating that entrance of the threads may take place very early in the formation of the essential organs of the flower. It is also a fact that by the time the flower parts are thrust into sight from the enfolding bases of the leaves the smut spores are in part fully developed and apparently ready for germination.

Unfortunately specimens showing the condition of the fungus after penetration of the essential organs but before spore formation were not preserved for examination, and so peculiarities of the mycelium, if such exist, immediately preceding spore formation can not be given here. However, examination of the very young spore bearing bodies, before all the mycelium has been changed into spores, has given information concerning some very interesting changes that take place in spore formation, and shows that in this species it is quite different from that attributed to Ustilago as a genus.

Evidently, after entrance into the essential organs, the formation of mycelium soon takes place most abundantly in the cells immediately beneath the epidermis, so that in time this becomes separated from the rest of the plant cells by a dense mass of fungous threads, which, as they multiply and change into spores, crowd inward the inclosed cells and stretch outward the layer of epidermal cells, the final result being the seed-like smutted part with its membrane on the outside, mass of spores within, and the columella in the center.

Sections through these infected bodies while quite young show the origin and character of these parts. Taking first the columella we find that it narrows somewhat irregularly from the base toward the apex and terminates before reaching the end of the spore bearing body. It forms a stiff, slender column that remains after the rest of the body has crumbled to pieces. If stamens go to make up part of the infected body but are made out as free bodies at the apex, the columella will send out a little branch into each of these originating from below where the stamen loses its identity with the main body; or if the stamens are entirely free from the ovary but still infected each will have its own columella. These columellas evidently are thus the fibrovascular parts and the undestroyed parenchyma cells that were intended for the formation of the essential organs of the flower. In stained sections they plainly show considerable of the sterile fungous threads ramifying through them.

Proceeding now to the membrane on the outside, the microscope shows that it is not entirely made up of the epidermal cells, but is rather a false membrane having on the outside the still more or less distinct epidermis, but beneath this a tissue of sterile fungous threads which forms its greater thickness. These sterile threads are quite different from the usual threads of the mycelium, especially when fully matured, and exhibit some variations in the hosts that belong to varieties other than broom-corn. The threads tend to break up into their component cells or short rows of these. The cells become rounded at their ends and assume a sub-spherical to irregular oblong shape. The walls are more or less thickened. Though usually empty they may contain some contents. The cell walls always retain their hyaline appearance and because of this and their large size and grouping together are in no way likely to be confused with the fertile spores that occur just beneath this membrane.

The sections also show that the spores are not formed simultaneously from the fertile threads that exist between the enveloping sterile cells of the membrane and the central plant cells of the columella, but that there is a progressive formation from without toward the columella or centripetally. It is quite probable, too, that this formation begins first at the free end, so that the oldest spores would be those near the top of the infected body. The formation of the spores so far as could be gathered from the youngest specimens at hand was as follows. Beginning next the columella the section presents an appearance as if the fungous threads had entirely gelatinized their walls, which, with the dissolved cell contents, formed a colorless amorphous stratum in which were imbedded the protoplasmic contents as very distinct, narrow and usually short and simple strands, almost bacteria-like in appearance. In these fine strands, less than a micron in diameter, are to be made out more highly refractive granules, possibly nuclear functioning bodies. As we proceed outward in the section the strands become irregularly contracted and apparently larger until we meet with those that are roundish and reforming a visible cell wall. Further out in the section the cell wall is more distinctly made out and becomes tinted. From here they grade into spores that are fully developed as to size, shape and color but are bound very closely together, while the outermost spores do not so firmly adhere to one another. The transformation is generally gradual, there being no sharp line of separation, that of color being most marked. There is more or less of a radial effect in the undeveloped parts, as if the formation was not entirely annular but as if various radial units had given origin to the formation but had more or less lost their individuality by lateral fusion. Perhaps projecting wedges of plant tissue give rise to this effect in part, but where these are apparently absent there are seen radial strands where the gelatinization of walls, etc., are not so marked. In the above manner gradually all of the spores are matured. When this has occurred, the spore mass dries out and becomes dusty, and the enveloping membrane sooner or later becomes ruptured and the spores are easily scattered by the wind.

From the above description it is seen that the spore formation is quite different from that usually described for Ustilago. However, an examination of very young outbreaks of *Ustilago* Zeæ (Beckm.) Unger in the leaves of corn showed that there is considerable resemblance. Here I found that frequently small groups of spores were formed from a mass of mycelium encircled on all sides by plant cells; and, while there was a less decided geletinization of walls and re-arrangement of protoplasmic strands, there was still a progression of spore development, though it was not nearly so marked as in broom-corn smut, and the central spores seemed to be the ones first formed. There were also threads more isolated in the plant tissue that were forming spores after the manner usually described for this genus. On the other hand an examination of Cintractia as described by Cornu[1] and Trelease,[2] and as exhibited by sections through rather mature specimens of *Cintractia axicola* and *Cintractia Junci* (species with which the above authors worked) shows that the fungus on broom-corn is a Cintractia, if that is entitled to generic distinction from Ustilago. In both of these species, as we found with broom-corn, there is a membrane composed of sterile cells and epidermis, but with them, unlike in broom-corn, the outbreak occurs just beneath the epidermis at the base of the flower peduncles; and, as the enclosed woody portion is normally developed, the strain of the spore formation of necessity ruptures the surrounding membrane and it soon falls off, leaving the spores naked but more or less agglutinated. These have been developed centripetally around the central cylinder of plant tissue, similarly to those of broom-corn smut around the columella. In *Cintractia axicola* there is also the radial effect but shown much more prominently. The germination of *Cintractia Junci* is somewhat similar, at least in water, to that of broom-corn smut. The place of outbreak and the appearance of the spores, however, in both these species is different from those of broom-corn.

[1] Ann. Sci. Nat. Bot VI. 15: 277–279. 1883.
[2] Bull. Torr. Bot. Club 12: 69–70. Jl. 1885.

### EXPERIMENTS.

*Object.* To determine some of the preceding facts concerning the life history of the fungus and also to find out whether it
was a trouble that could be prevented, it was necessary to carry
on a number of experiments with plants both in the laboratory and
in the field. The indoor experiments were along two lines. First,
to determine by infection the place or places on the broom-corn
through which the smut gains entrance. Second, to determine
the effect of hot water on the germination of the seeds of broom-
corn and of the spores of the fungus. The field experiments
were chiefly to compare the amount of smut produced in plants
whose seed was treated with hot water with that produced in
those whose seed was not treated.

*Infection experiments.* While many attempts were made to
infect plants by placing spores on the seed or on very young
parts of the germinating plants, the success of which was deter-
mined later by the presence of mycelium in the tissues, the per
cent. of plants that became infected was not very large. This was
doubtless due in part to the use of spores, instead of pure cultures
of sporidia of the right age for infection—the method used by
Brefeld. The spores, however, always germinated very easily and
abundantly, and it was thought they would furnish a source for
infection equal to that which exists in nature. The spores were
used also to determine, if possible, whether the fine threads of
the spores that we have called infection-threads were really of
that nature. The experiments were mostly made with seed treated
with hot water, and germinated in soil or sand free from spores.
The germinating seeds were then moistened at certain places, or
at certain ages, with water containing spores. After growth varying from a day or so to two or three weeks either the epidermis
was examined for evidences of penetration or sections were cut
and examined for mycelium.

It seems to be a fact that there is a close relationship between
the stage of germination of the spores and the place or age of the
parts through which infection takes place. These conditions
seemed to be best adjusted by placing the spores on the seed and
allowing both to germinate together in earth, at least most of the
plants that became infested were those so treated. Although many
trials were made by placing germinated or ungerminated spores
on the germs at various places and ages, we were not successful in
our examination of the epidermis afterward in finding spores or
sporidia on the outside that were connected with mycelium
within. It was a common thing, however, to find vigorously germinating spores in which there were no signs of the threads pene-

trating the epidermis. A few spores were found in one case where there seemed to be some attempt on the part of the infection-threads to push down between the cell walls of the epidermis. Mycelium, in the sections, was frequently found in the epidermal cells, in a few cases showing a narrowed part at the end of a thread as if entrance had been gained near that point (pl. 4, fig. 3). The mycelium was always most abundant in the region where epicotyl and leaf-sheath joined, and very little, if any, toward the seed end of the epicotyl. This would seem to indicate, at least in these cases, that if penetration took place through the epicotyl it did so very early, or only at the upper end if later. That it is largely a question of young tissue that can be penetrated easily is shown by the fact that plants that had one or two leaves through the sheath, but with this still fresh, became infected when this was removed and spores placed on the base of the exposed leaves where the cells were quite young; while plants not nearly so old did not become infected when spores were merely placed at a corresponding position but on the outside of the normally exposed parts of the sheath, the cells there being more mature. In the field experiments where spores were placed on young leaves at different ages of the plants, it was shown that successful infection did not take place in these cases, probably, because even if penetration was successful, the threads were not able to reach the growing tip.

*Effect of treatment on seed.* In the treatment with hot water it was desired to find out at what temperature the treatment began to injure the germinative power of the seeds, how much higher this temperature is than that at which the spores are killed, and whether this difference, if any, was great enough to permit of the treatment as a practical operation. Two vessels of water were used—one at about the required temperature in which the seeds in a small bag were placed to take off the chill, and the other at the desired constant temperature, in which the seeds were immersed for the required time. The thermometer was placed inside the bag so that it would register the temperature of the water immediately surrounding the seeds. After treatment one hundred seeds were selected and, with a similar number of untreated as a check, were placed in a Geneva germinator. Every twenty-four hours all seeds that had germinated were removed and the number noted.

In the following table the results of the treatments are given. In some cases the same treatment was tried twice but at different times of the year. The different lots were treated at various times during the fall and winter and germinated in a room where there was some variation of temperature. The conditions for each treated lot and its check were, however, exactly the same. From the table it will be seen that there was practically no difference between the treated and untreated lots up to the temperature of 132° F., and 135° F. for ten minutes. From here on there was somewhat of a retardation of germination. The treatment at 140° F. and higher seems on some occasions also to have killed some few seeds. These results, of course, might vary with the seed used—the older the seed the less likely it would be to stand the higher temperatures; different varieties might vary slightly in resistance power; seeds freed from their glumes would be injured more easily than seed tightly invested by the glumes. The results, however, show that broom-corn seed has a resistance power against hot water higher than that of our other common agricultural grasses, and consequently there would be less chance of injury to the seed in the treatment, other conditions being the same

GERMINATION OF BROOM-CORN SEED TREATED WITH HOT WATER.

| Treatment of seeds. | | Hours after placing in germinator. | | | | | | | | | | | % Germ. | % failed. |
|---|---|---|---|---|---|---|---|---|---|---|---|---|---|---|
| | | 24 | 48 | 72 | 96 | 120 | 144 | 168 | 192 | 216 | 240 | 264 | | |
| Seeds in hot water, 120° F. for 15 min. | Treated | 0 | 13 | 47 | 21 | 5 | 6 | 5 | | | | | 97 | 3 |
| | Check | 0 | 11 | 61 | 19 | 1 | 0 | 4 | | | | | 96 | 4 |
| Seeds in hot water, 130° F. for 5 min. | Treated | 2 | 8 | | 63 | 14 | 2 | 2 | 4 | | | | 95 | 5 |
| | Check | 4 | 10 | | 64 | 12 | 2 | 2 | 2 | | | | 96 | 4 |
| Seeds in hot water, 130° F. for 10 min. | Treated | 1 | 5 | 76 | | 8 | 3 | 1 | 2 | | | | 96 | 4 |
| | Check | 0 | 6 | 82 | | 5 | 0 | 3 | 2 | | | | 98 | 2 |
| Seeds in hot water, 130° F. for 15 min. | Treated | 2 | 7 | 60 | 18 | 9 | | | | | | | 96 | 4 |
| | Check | 1 | 2 | 55 | 37 | 1 | | | | | | | 96 | 4 |
| Seeds in hot water, 130° F. for 15 min. | Treated | 0 | 8 | 30 | 28 | 13 | 8 | 2 | | 2 | 1 | 3 | 95 | 5 |
| | Check | 0 | 8 | 36 | 30 | 13 | 5 | 2 | | 2 | 2 | 2 | 100 | 0 |
| Seeds in hot water, 132° F. for 5 min. | Treated | 1 | 18 | 50 | | 23 | 3 | | | | | | 95 | 5 |
| | Check | 0 | 23 | 51 | | 18 | 2 | | | | | | 94 | 6 |
| Seeds in hot water, 132° F. for 10 min. | Treated | 0 | 8 | 44 | 24 | 14 | 7 | 0 | 1 | | | | 98 | 2 |
| | Check | 0 | 29 | 34 | 22 | 5 | 7 | 1 | 1 | | | | 99 | 1 |
| Seeds in hot water, 135° F. for 5 min. | Treated | 0 | 12 | 33 | 24 | 19 | 6 | 3 | 1 | 2 | | | 100 | 0 |
| | Check | 1 | 16 | 34 | 19 | 14 | 5 | 1 | 0 | 3 | 2 | | 95 | 5 |
| Seeds in hot water, 135° F. for 10 min. | Treated | 0 | 2 | 33 | 27 | 18 | 3 | 5 | 3 | 2 | | | 93 | 7 |
| | Check | 0 | 17 | 37 | 25 | 6 | 6 | 0 | 0 | 1 | | | 92 | 8 |
| Seeds in hot water, 135° F. for 15 min. | Treated | 3 | 50 | 25 | | 10 | 5 | 5 | 1 | | | | 99 | 1 |
| | Check | 3 | 67 | 12 | | 7 | 5 | 1 | 1 | | | | 96 | 4 |
| Seeds in hot water, 135° F. for 15 min. | Treated | 1 | 5 | 34 | 26 | | 13 | 8 | 5 | 1 | 2 | 1 | 96 | 4 |
| | Check | 0 | 8 | 51 | 24 | | 12 | 5 | 0 | 0 | 0 | | 100 | 0 |
| Seeds in hot water, 140° F. for 15 min. | Treated | 2 | 12 | 23 | | 17 | 10 | 9 | 4 | | | | 77 | 23 |
| | Check | 3 | 67 | 12 | | 7 | 5 | 1 | 1 | | | | 96 | 4 |
| Seeds in hot water, 150° F. for 15 min. | Treated | 1 | 28 | | 41 | 11 | 5 | 2 | | | | | 85 | 12 |
| | Check | 11 | 60 | | 17 | 7 | 2 | 1 | | | | | 98 | 2 |
| Seeds in hot water, 150° F. for 15 min. | Treated | 0 | 2 | 22 | 31 | | 25 | 8 | 2 | 3 | 0 | 2 | 95 | 5 |
| | Check | 0 | 6 | 43 | 23 | | 17 | 5 | 1 | 0 | 2 | 0 | 97 | 3 |

*Effect of treatment on spores.* The effect of hot water on the germination of the spores was studied at the same time. Smutted seed-like bodies (broken and entire) were placed with the seed to be treated, also spores placed on the inner surface of a small piece of paper that was folded once. In the last case the spores were placed on the paper in order that they could be found after treatment, and were supposed to be subjected to the same temperature as spores that might occur on the surface of seeds. Possibly the paper furnished some little protection against the heat, but certainly not so much as would be furnished those spores that had slipped down between the glumes of the seeds. After treatment some of the spores from the interior of unbroken smutted bodies, from the broken ones and from the paper, together with untreated spore as a check, were placed in water in culture cells and examined with the microscope from time to time to determine the amount and time of their germination. The results, abbreviated from the notes taken at the time, are as follows :

No. 1028. In hot water 130° F. for 5 min.; spores taken from inside of unbroken body. Examined 17 hours after placing in culture cells, and found spores germinating very actively, probably from 50 to 75 per cent.; stage of germination possibly not quite so far advanced as in the check.

No. 1029. Treatment same ; spores from surface of paper. Examined same time as above, and found not over one or two per cent. germinating and these much behind stage of development of those in the check.

No. 1030. Check, or spores not treated. When examined with above found nearly every spore germinating and most of them quite far advanced.

Later examination showed little change in the relative amounts of germination of the above.

No. 1035. In hot water 130° F. for 10 min.; spores from inside of unbroken body. Examined 24 hours after placing in culture cells, and found about 5 per cent. had germinated and these in about the same stage as check spores.

No. 1034. Treatment same; spores from surface of paper. At end of 24 hours about 3 per cent. had germinated and these were not so far advanced as in check.

No. 1036. Check. About 50 per cent. had germinated and these well advanced. Have no data as to later examinations and conditions.

No. 1045. In hot water 132° F. for 10 min.; spores from inside of body. Examined 24 hours after placing in culture cells and found less than a dozen germinating spores. At end of 48 hours, however, the spores had germinated abundantly, though not so abundantly as in check. A second culture made 24 hours after treatment and taken from a different infected body that had quite a tough and unbroken membrane showed no retardation in germination at the end of 24 hours, and also had about as many spores germinating as in the check lot.

No. 1044. Treatment same ; spores from surface of paper. Results the same as in first example of 1045.

No. 1046. Check. At end of 24 hours germinated spores were very abundant and very well advanced.

No. 1049. In hot water 134°-5° F. for 5 min.; spores from inside of an unbroken and firmly covered body. Examined at end of 24 hours and found germination well advanced, and even more abundant than in check slide.

No. 1048. Treatment same; spores from surface of paper. At end of 24 hours only a spore or two had germinated; at end of 48 hours a few more had germinated; at end of 65 hours quite a few extra were beginning to germinate, though altogether not over 5 or 10 per cent.

No. 1050. Check. At end of 24 hours germination was abundant, though perhaps exceeded in 1049.

No. 1051. In hot water 135° F. for 10 min.; spores from center of unbroken body. At end of 24 hours examined and found the spores were germinating as well in all respects as in check. The covering of the infected body had protected these central spores so that they had not become wet, and the treatment if anything had done them good.

No. 1052. Treatment same; spores from the same body but near the surface. These spores had been wet by the water, and while their germination was retarded somewhat and was not so abundant as the above, it was still quite vigorous.

No. 1053. Treatment same; spores from surface of paper. At end of 24 hours less than a dozen spores had germinated out of the many hundreds present.

No. 1054. Treatment same; spores from inside a punctured body. At end of 24 hours did not find any germinating spores. Later on about a dozen germinating spores were found.

No. 1055. Check. At end of 24 hours the spores had germinated very abundantly; condition about as in 1051.

At end of four days the per cent. of germination in the above had not increased to any appreciable extent.

No. 1103. In hot water 135° F. for 15 min.; spores from center of an unbroken body. Examined at end of 24 hours and found the spores had begun to germinate abundantly.

No. 1102. Treatment same; spores from surface of paper. None of these spores germinated.

This experiment was tried twice with about the same results. A nutrient fluid was used as the medium in this case.

No. 1107. In hot water 150° F. for 15 min., spores from center of unbroken seed. No spores germinated.

No. 1106. Treatment same; spores from surface of paper. No spores germinated.

These experiments show that a short treatment with warm water has no injurious effect, may possibly even be beneficial to the germination of the spores. As the temperature of the water is increased, however, it shows a retarding influence on the germination. Closely associated with retarded development is the fatal effect of the hot water. In general, a direct exposure in water at 130°–132° F. for five or ten minutes showed a retarding and with some spores a fatal effect. A direct exposure for fifteen minutes in water at 135° F. is almost certain to prove fatal to all of the spores. Spores, however, in the unbroken bodies can stand immersion in water of a higher temperature, the degree depending upon the thickness or impenetrability of the membrane to the water.

It was shown in the treatment of broom-corn seed that an exposure at 140° F. for fifteen minutes may be taken as the lower limit at which we may begin to look for bad effects from the treat-

ment of good seed. This gives a greater safety range than we
have in the similar treatment for the smut of oats or wheat. Perfect results in preventing the smut can not always be expected
with seed in which there are many unbroken infected kernels,
as the treatment (135° F. for fifteen minutes) will not be severe
enough to kill all of the spores, and subsequent handling may
break the kernels and scatter the spores among the seed. It is
quite possible, also, that spores that have worked down between
the glumes are sometimes protected sufficiently to withstand this
treatment and are able to infect the germinating plant. These
conditions probably account for the imperfect results obtained in
some of the following experiments where a large amount of smut
was mixed with the seed before treatment.

At the same time that the heat experiments were conducted a
few were tried to determine the influence of cold. Are the conditions of winter weather such as would kill spores in infected
canes left outdoors on the ground? The germination of some
spores that had been so treated was tried in the spring. Only one
trial was made but this failed to show any germinating spores.
However, they all presented the appearance as if they had germinated before, which was quite likely the case. The germination
of spores subjected to the following conditions was also tried :

    No. 1060.  Spores on ice for 15 minutes.
    No. 1061.  Check culture.
    No. 1062.  Spores on ice for one hour.
    No. 1063.  Spores in ice-water for four hours.

At the end of 24 hours after placing in culture cells, all the
above had germinated abundantly, showing no difference at that
time or later.

*Field experiments, 1894.* During this year experiments were
first undertaken to prevent broom-corn from smutting. Two lots
of seed, one ordinary seed and the other quite smutty, were di-
vided into three parts, a treatment with hot water and with a solution of copper sulphate being given to two of the parts of each
lot and the third parts left untreated. The seed, however, was
planted so late that the broom-corn did not have time to com-
pletely form its panicles before it was killed by frost. A careful examination of the immature panicles that had appeared
showed but three smutted ones, and those all from the untreated
lot of badly smutted seed. In this plat one hundred twenty-five
plants were advanced enough to examine the panicles. The conditions were not such as to give trustworthy results and no conclusions could be had.

*Field experiments, 1895.*  This year the experiments were considerably widened so as to include not only experiments in preventing and increasing smut in the plants but also one to determine whether plants could become infected by spores carried
to the tender parts above ground.  The conditions and results of
these experiments are given in the table for 1895.  From this it
will be seen that experiments 1 and 2 were conducted at Arcola,
Ill., which is in the principal broom-corn district of the state.
The seed, however, was planted on land that had not been in
broom-corn before.  Unfortunately the broom-corn was cut a few
days before the writer examined it, but the smutted heads had
been left behind and so could be counted, while the total was
easily obtained from standing bases of the canes.  The remaining
experiments were conducted at Urbana, Ill., out of the broom-
corn district and on land that had never been in broom-corn before.  In all cases the smut used was such that germinated readily
in water.  In the last experiment the spores were in water that
was squirted on the young unrolled parts when the plants aver-
aged about six inches high.

FIELD EXPERIMENTS WITH BROOM-CORN SMUT, 1895.

| No. | Conditions of the experiments. | Smutty. | Free. | Total. | % Smutty. |
|---|---|---|---|---|---|
| 1. | Seed mixed with smut; no treat-ment.  At Arcola, Ill........... | 40 | 760 | 800 | 5. |
| 2. | Seed mixed with smut; treated with hot water 135° F. for 15 min.  At Arcola, Ill.................. | 2 | 798 | 800 | 0.25 |
| 3. | Ordinary seed; no treatment....... | 20 | 1183 | 1203 | 1.66 |
| 4. | Seed mixed with smut; no treatment. | 126 | 1074 | 1200 | 10.5 |
| 5. | Seed treated with hot water 135° F. for 15 min.; mixed with smut two years old..................... | 174 | 1072 | 1246 | 14. |
| 6. | Seed mixed with smut; treated with hot water 135° F. for 15 min..... | 2 | 927 | 929 | 0.21 |
| 7. | Seed mixed with smut; treated with hot water 140° F. for 15 min..... | 1 | 1320 | 1321 | 0.07 |
| 8. | Seed mixed with smut; placed in water to skim off smutted kernels; treated with hot water 135° F. for 15 min.................. | 0 | 1168 | 1168 | 0. |
| 9. | Seed treated with hot water 135° F. for 15 min.; smut placed on young plants soon after coming up...... | 1 | 1314 | 1315 | 0.07 |

These experiments show that in every case where used the
hot water practically prevented the smut, no matter whether ordinary or very smutty seed had been so treated.  Also that whereas

the ordinary seed gave less than 2 per cent. of smutted plants, this was increased to 10 and 14 per cent. when very smutty seed was used; that smut two years old which had been kept in a dry place had lost none of its power to infect plants. Lastly it was shown that smut in these plants was not increased by spores being placed on the young parts above ground. Before drawing conclusions from these experiments, the conclusions from which seemed so evident, it was desired to repeat them another year, and add others suggested by them.

*Field experiments, 1896.* The experiments this year were all made at Urbana, the ground that had been used the year before and a new piece being had for the two sets of experiments. With the ground that had been in broom-corn the previous year, the aim was two-fold. First, to determine the relation of smut in the land to the amount of smut in the crop; and second, to test again the value of hot water treatment.

In table 1 for 1896 is given a diagram of the way the land was platted during the two years. The dark lines indicate the boundary of the land. In 1895 the seven plats, 3–9, ran cross-wise, while in 1896 the four plats, a–d, extended lengthwise of the same. From the table it will be seen that in 1895 plats 4 and 5 bore by far the smuttiest crop; but as most of the smutty panicles were removed before much of the smut was shed, there was perhaps not much that reached the ground in any plat. However, to make a difference, in the fall of 1895 a large amount of smut was dusted from the panicles all over plat 4 and the smutted panicles were placed on this plat. There could be no doubt that this plat contained a good deal of smut and that at least plats 8 and 9 had very little if any. If smut in the land was one of the means of infecting a crop, then the plants in the four plats of 1896 might be expected to show the most smut where they crossed plat 4 of 1895. In the table the total number of stalks, the number of smutted ones, and the per cent. of smutted ones that were found in the experiment of 1896 are given for each of the areas formed by the cross platting of the two years. A glance at this will show that plat 4 in none of the four treatments gave evidence of an increased per cent. of smut over the rest of the land having seed treated the same. This, taken with the fact that in plat a, where the seed was treated and there was no smut in any of the areas, would indicate that smutty land is not an important factor in producing a smutty crop.

The second aim of the experiment, to determine the effect of hot water treatment, is shown in the column of totals for the four treatments. Ordinary seed treated with hot water gave a crop

TABLE I.—FIELD EXPERIMENTS WITH BROOM-CORN, 1896.

| Plats. 1896. | Treatment in 1896. | Panicles. | 1.6%, '95. | 10.5%, '95. | 14%, '95. | .2%, '95. | .07%, '95. | 0%, '95. | .07%, '95. | Totals. |
|---|---|---|---|---|---|---|---|---|---|---|
| d. | Seed mixed with smut; no treatment | Number. | 306 | 209 | 323 | 314 | 330 | 300 | 450 | 2232 |
|  |  | Smutty. | 82 | 60 | 96 | 93 | 80 | 82 | 132 | 625 |
|  |  | Per cent. | 27 | 29 | 30 | 30 | 24 | 27 | 29 | 28 |
| c. | Ordinary seed; no treatment | Number. | 282 | 297 | 419 | 354 | 460 | 345 | 686 | 2843 |
|  |  | Smutty. | 13 | 4 | 10 | 19 | 14 | 14 | 25 | 99 |
|  |  | Per cent. | 4.6 | 1.3 | 2.3 | 5.3 | 3. | 4. | 3.6 | 3.4 |
| b. | Seed mixed with smut; treated with hot water 135° F. for 15 minutes | Number. | 260 | 394 | 380 | 339 | 387 | 246 | 423 | 2429 |
|  |  | Smutty. | 6 | 18 | 21 | 16 | 12 | 11 | 22 | 106 |
|  |  | Per cent. | 2.0 | 4.5 | 5.5 | 4.7 | 3.1 | 4.4 | 5.2 | 4.3 |
| a. | Ordinary seed; treated with hot water about 135° F. for 15 minutes | Number. | 332 | 281 | 324 | 300 | 349 | 275 | 239 | 2400 |
|  |  | Smutty. | 0 | 0 | 0 | 0 | 0 | 0 | 0 | 0 |
|  |  | Per cent. | 0 | 0 | 0 | 0 | 0 | 0 | 0 | 0 |
|  | Plats in 1895 |  | 3. | 4. | 5. | 6. | 7. | 8. | 9. | Totals. |

entirely free from smut, while the crop from the same lot of seed but not treated had nearly three and a half per cent. of the panicles smutted. In the case where smut was mixed with the seed

the part that was afterward treated with hot water produced a crop
that only had four and one-third per cent. of the panicles smutted,
while the untreated part gave a crop of which twenty-eight per
cent. was smutted. The results of treatment, then, were the same
as in the previous year, save that in the case of the badly smutted
seed the prevention of smut was not quite so complete. This can
be explained on the assumption that the treatment was not severe
enough to kill all the spores (spores in the inside of smutted kernels or possibly some of those that had slipped down between the
glumes of sound seed) and by the fact that here it was an unusually good year for the development of smut, as is shown by the
large amount given for the plats of these and the next experiments.

The second set of experiments made in 1896, as was stated,
was on land that had never before been in broom-corn, and
included beside the preventive experiments (as a check on the
preceding set) a few to determine the possibility of infecting
young plants of different ages by placing spores on them. The
results are embodied in the following table.

TABLE 2. FIELD EXPERIMENTS WITH BROOM-CORN, 1896.

| Plat. | Conditions of the experiments. | Smutty. | Free. | Total. | Per cent. |
|---|---|---|---|---|---|
| A. | Ordinary seed; treated with hot water 133°–135° F. for 15 min.... | 2 | 1675 | 1677 | 0.12 |
| B. | Seed mixed with smut; treated with hot water 135° F. for 15 min..... | 360 | 1128 | 1488 | 24. |
| C. | Ordinary seed; no treatment....... | 357 | 1536 | 1893 | 19. |
| D. | Seed mixed with smut; no treatment. | 495 | 565 | 1050 | 47. |
| E. | Seed treated with hot water 133°–135° F. for 15 min.; smut placed on young plants before appearing above ground................. | 8 | 106 | 114 | 7. |
| F * | Seed treated with hot water 133°–135° F. for 15 min.; smut placed on young plants just after appearing above ground...... .... | 1 | 345 | 346 | 0.3 |
| G.* | Seed treated with hot water 133°–135° F. for 15 min.; smut placed on plants when about two feet high. ..................... | 0 | 420 | 420 | 0. |
| H † | Quite smutty seed of the season of 1893..... .... ............ | 509 | 481 | 990 | 51. |

Examination of this table shows that hot water treatment of
ordinary seed has again given the uniform result of the preven-

* Seed of all the plants was planted May 27. Smut in water was squirted on the
young unrolled parts of the plants in plat F. on June 13, while in plat G. the same operation was performed on July 9.

† A different variety of broom-corn seed than that used in any other experiment in
1895 or 1896, but from the same lot of seed as was used in 1894.

tion of smut. The same seed untreated gave an unusually large number of smutted plants, nineteen per cent. With the seed mixed with smut the treated part showed less favorable results than in any of the previous similar experiments, but still there is a very decided difference between it and the untreated part, which had over fifty per cent., or twice as much. The placing of smut on very young plants before they came above the ground gave rise to a few smutty plants, but the percentage was not nearly so great as it would have been had the smut been placed on seeds instead. Placing smut on the young parts after the plants had appeared above the ground gave results similar to a previous experiment—no increase in smut.

The results of the three years are thus seen to be quite uniform, always showing favorable for the treatment. The only seeming exception is in the case of treatment of very badly smutted seed. Here the treatment was not severe enough to kill all of the smut spores, and the varying favorable conditions of the different years or ground used gave rise to a varying amount of smut, though never to nearly so great a per cent. as in the same seed untreated.

*Prevention experiments elsewhere.* In the literature of the smuts of the sorghum group of plants the only prevention experiments we have come across are those conducted in 1891 by Kellerman at the Experiment Station of Kansas. With *Ustilago Sorghi* of sorghum he tried seed treatment with different strengths of solution and time of immersion of potassium sulphid and chlorid of iron, and also with hot water. The check plats gave such a small per cent. of smutted plants that the author drew no conclusions from the results of his experiments. In the two cases where he used hot water, however, he had no smutted plants. It is stated that at the Khandesh Experiment Farm,[1] of India, season of 1892, copper sulphate treatment of seed was used with good results in preventing a common smut of sorghum.

### EFFECT OF ENVIRONMENT ON PARASITE AND HOST.

*Some interrogations.* What are the environmental conditions favorable or unfavorable for the infection of a plant by the smut and for the development of the latter afterward? Such conditions may be quite general or quite specific. Some years or certain localities give rise to badly smutted crops and we say the general conditions have been favorable for such and usually ascribe such conditions to the presence of spores with the seeds and to the

---

[1] Exp. Stat. Rec. **5**: 354.

warm moist weather at the infection period.  But there are other
more specific, perhaps largely indeterminable, conditions than
these that might have an influence in determining the per cent. of
smut that appears in the plants.  Take, for instance, very smutty
seed; why does it in two succeeding years in the same locality
show the variation from ten (plat 4, '95) to forty-seven (plat D, '96)
per cent.?  Given the same ordinary seed planted but a few days
apart on plats but a short distance from each other; why does it
show the variation from three (plat c, '96) to nineteen (plat C, '96)
per cent.?  In 1894 smutty seed a year old was planted so late that
the plants showed but a few immature panicles before they were
killed by the frost.  A careful examination for smut in the one
hundred and twenty-five panicles that appeared gave three with
evidence of smut.  The same lot of seed planted at the proper
time in 1896 gave over fifty (plat H, '96) per cent. of smutted panicles.  What were the causes of this difference?  Or to make the
case extremely specific in the same lot of seed in the same plat
we have one stalk smutted and another free.  Why?

*Environment before infection.*  While we are not able now to
cite each case to its cause or causes, yet we may give certain conditions that seem to have a greater or less bearing.  Such fall into
two groups; namely, those that are favorable or unfavorable to
infection of the host by the fungus, and those that affect the relationship of the two after infection.  Take two seeds, for instance,
and the soil immediately surrounding each.  One or more of the
following differences in condition might determine why one
became infected and the other not: number and germinative character of the spores present; amount of water present; character of
the gases in the soil and water; chemical character of the soluble
parts of the soil; bacterial development as unfavorable for prolific germination of spores; nutrient solutions formed from manure
and decayed vegetable matter as a source for prolific formation of
sporidia; movement of water as a means of bringing germs to
infection-area of the germinating seed; heat in the presence and
absence of moisture.  Or the conditions of the seeds themselves
possibly might aid in deciding the matter; namely, age of seed
as affecting character and vitality of germination and these in turn
favorable or not for the germs present; individual character or
vitality of different seeds; heat and moisture as affecting rapidity
of germination and character of tissue formed; depth of planting,
etc. as affecting length and character of epicotyl and leaf-sheath.

*Environment after infection.*  Brefeld has shown that certain
smuts sometimes succeed in entering their host but still do not
succeed in forming spores.  In the case at hand the fungus suc-

ceeds in entering the germinating plantlet say in June, while the spore masses do not become visible in the flower parts of the same until between two and three months later. May there not be conditions developed during this time that are favorable to the one and not to the other? May not outside conditions of heat and moisture or peculiar hereditary character of individual plants favor the formation of plant tissue having great resistance to the penetrating threads of the fungus, thus conquering it, or the reverse? May not the growing point of the plant outstrip in upward growth the fungous threads and thus cut them off from further development? Would not tardy invasion of the floral parts prevent or lessen the spore formation? This latter question can be answered in the affirmative, if we count the evidence presented by flowers with more or less of their parts infected or of panicles with only part of the flowers infected, apparently the earlier developed being free. Such conditions and results are, however, with our present knowledge largely matters of speculation.

## HISTORICAL REVIEW.

*Bibliography.* The following list includes all of the articles that the writer has been able to find in which mention of this smut is made. The references are reported by the name of the fungus used rather than by the general title of the article, except when the article especially treats of the fungus.

BARY, A. de. *Ustilago Tulasnei.* Vergleich. Morph. u. Biol. der Pilze Mycet. u. Bact. 369. 1884.
> Gives Liebenberg as authority for germination of spores after being in herbarium six and a half years.

BESSEY, C. E. *Ustilago Sorghi* (Link) Pass. Neb. Farmer 14: 189. 6 Mr. 1890.
> Notes its appearance in Nebraska, and recommends blue-vitriol treatment of seed.

BREFELD, O. *Ustilago Tulasnei* Kühn auf *Sorghum vulgare.* Untersuch. aus dem Gesammt. der Mykol. 12: 120–122. *pl. 7. f. 19–22.* 1895.
> Gives culture experiments, etc. with this fungus.

BURRILL, T. J. *Ustilago Sorghi* (Link) Winter. Proc. Am. Soc. Micr. 1888:—(12).
> Lists this smut from Illinois.

COMES, O. *Ustilago Tulasnei* Kühn. Crittog. Agr. 75. 1891.
> Gives brief note as to hosts, etc.

DE-TONI, J. B. *Ustilago Sorghi* (Link) Pass. Syll. Fung. $7^1$: 456. 25 O. 1888.
> Gives description, hosts, synonyms, etc.

EVANS, W. H. Sorghum Smuts. Handb. Exp. Stat. Work. 326. 1893.
> Gives a brief note on *U. sorghi.*

FAILYER, G. H., and WILLARD, J. T. Smut in Sorghum. Exp. Stat. Kans. St. Agr. Coll. 16: 145. 1891.
> Mention finding two kinds of smut on imported varieties of sorghum.

FARLOW, W. G., and SEYMOUR, A. B. *Ustilago Sorghi* (Lk.) Pass. Prov. Host-Index Fungi U. S. 154. Je. 1891.
Give as hosts *Sorghum saccharatum* and *S. vulgare*.

FISCHER DE WALDHEIM, A *Tilletia Sorghi-vulgaris*, Tul. Pringsh. Jahrb. 7. 106, 111. 1869.—(Transl. N. Y. St. Agr. Soc. **1870**: 280. 1871.)
Lists this fungus.

FISCHER DE WALDHEIM, A. *Ustilago Tulasnei*, Kühn. Aperçu System. des Ustil. 12. 1877.—(Hedw. **16**: 101. Jl. 1877.)
Gives brief description with synonyms.

FRANK, A. B. *Ustilago Tulasnei*, Kühn. Die Krankh. der Pflanz. 431. 1880.
Gives brief description, distribution, etc.

FRIES, E. *Sporisorium Sorghi*. Syst. Mycol. **3**: 454-5. 1832.
Gives botanical description of the fungus copied from Link.

KELLERMAN, W. A., and SWINGLE, W. T Notes on Sorghum Smuts. Proc. Kans' Acad. Sci. **12**: 158. 1890.
Note distribution of *Ustilago Sorghi* in U. S. and give hosts in Kansas.

KELLERMAN, W. A. Experiments with Sorghum Smuts. Exp. Stat. Kans. St. Agr. Coll. **23**: 95-101. *pl. 2*. Ag. 1891.
Gives descriptions of *U. Sorghi* and *U. Reiliana* and results of infection and prevention experiments.

KÜHN, J. Die Brandformen der Sorghum-Arten, *Tilletia Sorghi*, Tul. and *Ustilago cruenta*, Kühn. Hamb. Gart. u. Blumenzeit. **28**: 177-8. 1872.
Briefly discusses the two forms, of which *U. cruenta* is described as new.

KÜHN, J. *Ustilago Tulasnei*, Kühn. Sitz. nat. Ges. Halle **1874**.—(Bot. Zeit. **32**: 122. 20 F. 1874.)
States that germination, etc. shows the fungus to be an Ustilago rather than a Tilletia.

KÜHN, J. Die Brandformen der Sorghumarten. Mittheil. d. Vereins f. Erdkunde. **1877**.—(Hedw. **17**: 6-14. Ja. 1878.)
Gives differences between the smuts so far found on Sorghum, of which *U. Tulasnei* is named as one.

LINK, H. F. *Sporisorium Sorghi*. Linn. Sp. Plant. **6**[2]: 86. 1825. [ed. Willd.]
Describes a specimen from Egypt on *Sorghum vulgare*, being the first printed account of our fungus.

LUERSSEN, C. *Ustilago Tulasnei*, Kühn. Handb. der System. Bot. **1**: 250. 1879.
Gives brief specific characters.

NORTON, J. B. S. *Ustilago Sorghi* (Link) Pass. Trans. Acad. Sci. St. Louis 7: 231, *pl. 25. f. 1-5*. 9 N. 1896.
Gives note on germination.

OUDEMANS, C. A. J. A. *Tilletia Sorghi*, Tull. Archiv. Neerl. **8**: 361. 1873.
Notes the finding of this at Utrecht in 1871.

PRILLIEUX, E. *Ustilago Sorghi* (Lk.) Pass. Bull. Soc. Bot. France 42: 30-30. *f. a-c*. Ja. 1895.
Gives structural details of infected body.

RABENHORST, L. *Tilletia Sorghi*, Tul. Hedw. **10**: 18. 1871.
Notes the collection of the fungus at Kardistan in the orient.

SCHROETER, J. *Ustilago Sorghi* (Link). Krypt. Flora v. Schlesien 3[1]: 267. 1889.
Gives description and synonyms.

SORAUER, P. *Tilletia Sorghi vulgaris.* Handb. Pflanzenkrankh. 259. 1874
　　Makes allusion to this fungus.

THÜMEN, F. de. *Ustilago Sorghi,* Pass. Hedw. 12: 114. Ag. 1873.
　　Gives description of this as a new species with Passerini as the authority.

TRELEASE, W. *Ustilago Sorghi* (Link). Trans. Wis. Acad. Sci. Arts. Letters 6:
　　—1886.—(Prelim. List Par. Fungi Wis. 34. N. 1884.
　　Notes distribution of the fungus in America.

TULASNE, L. R. *Tilletia Sorghi-vulgaris.* Ann. Sci. Nat. Bot. III. 7: 116. *p. 5. f. 17-22.* 1847.
　　Describes this species under above name.

WEBBER, H. J. *Ustilago Sorghi* (Link) Pass. Agr. Exp. Stat. Neb. 1*: 69. 18 D. 1889.
　　—(Ann. Rep. Neb. St. Bd. Agr. 1889: 214. 1890.)
　　Notes occurrence of this fungus in Nebraska.

WINTER, G. *Ustilago Sorghi* (Link). Rabenh. Krypt. Flora 1: 90. 1884. [2nd ed.]
　　Gives specific description, synonyms, etc.

*Exsiccati.* Specimens of the fungus have been distributed under the following names in the quoted exsiccati.

　　*Ustilago Sorghi,* Pass. Thümen Herbarium mycologicum œconomicum *63.* 1873.
　　*Ustilago Tulasnei,* Kühn. Rabenhorst Fungi Europaei *1997.* 1875?
　　*Ustilago Sorghi* (Lk.) Wint. Ellis North American Fungi *1496.* 1885.
　　*Ustilago Sorghi* (Lk.). Briosi & Cavara Funghi parassiti delle piante coltivate od utile *28.* 1889.
　　*Ustilago Sorghi* (Link) Wint. Roumeguère Fungi selecti exsiccati *5128.* 1890.

*Nomenclature.* So far as can be gathered from the preceding references the history of the fungus is as follows: In 1825 Link published under the name of *Sporisorium Sorghi* a smut on a variety of sorghum gathered in Egypt and communicated by Ehrenberg. The fact that the description given is not minute and the further fact that several smuts have since been found on the same host tend to make it uncertain whether this description refers to what is now commonly called *Ustilago Sorghi* or not. This uncertainty, however, is dispelled by the existence of the original specimen in the Berlin Herbarium, where it was examined by Kühn and found to be this fungus. The next reference to this species that could be found, aside from the copied description of Link by Fries in 1832, is under the title of *Tilletia Sorghi-vulgaris* by Tulasne in 1847. This specific name has been abbreviated by some authors into *Tilletia Sorghi.* In 1874, however, Kühn showed that the germination of this fungus put it in the genus Ustilago rather than Tilletia, and he renamed it *Ustilago Tulasnei.* In the meantime, in 1873, another supposedly new species of smut on sorghum was described under the name of *Ustilago Sorghi.* Although issued by de Thümen in his exsiccati and described by him in *Hedwigia,* he gave Passerini, the collector, as authority for the name. Fischer de Waldheim in 1877 placed this name as a synonym of *U. Tulasnei,* thus regarding the former fungus as not

distinct. Winter (in Die Pilze) seems to have been the first to
have placed the smut in the genus Ustilago and at the same time
to have used the earliest specific name applied and the authority,
namely, *Ustilago Sorghi* (Link), for the same.

However, our study of the reproduction of the fungus shows
it to be a Cintractia. This would make the present name *Cintractia Sorghi* but for the fact that De-Toni has already referred
the Sorokine fungus (*Endothlaspis Sorghi*) questioningly to this
genus as *Cintractia? Sorghi* (Sorok.), thus making a fungus already
of that name. So far as we can learn the identity of this latter
fungus has not yet been further worked out, either as to its
generic position or its relationship to the smuts already reported
on the sorghum-like plants; yet from what we can gather from
the anatomical description and figures given by Sorokine it agrees
in general with our fungus, thus increasing the belief that it is a
Cintractia. To avoid confusion with the species of Sorokine,
however, we present the second specific name applied to the fungus we are considering, the name used by Tulasne, which gives
the following arrangement, *Cintractia Sorghi-vulgaris* (Tul.).

## SUMMARY.

1. Broom-corn smut is a parasite belonging to the lowest
group of plants called fungi. On the plants very closely related
to broom-corn this and several other smuts have been found. As
is shown by its spore formation, this smut really belongs to the
genus Cintractia rather than to Ustilago, to which it has of late
years been referred, and *Cintractia Sorghi-vulgaris* (Tul.) is the
name suggested for it.

2. Broom-corn infected with this fungus produces, as a usual
thing, brush of a very inferior quality, the rays being scattered
on a large central axis instead of having a common point of origin. Seed formation is also prevented by the fungus forming
its spores in the young ovaries and stamens. Brush gathered with
moisture on it may have these spores settle in this and stick to
the brush when it dries, thus affecting its appearance. The
thrashing of infected brush is disagreeable because of the dust
formed by the fungous spores.

3. Broom-corn only becomes successfully infected by the
fungus while the seeds germinate. The fungus succeeds at that
time in penetrating the very young tissues usually before the
plant issues above the ground, and the fungous threads which
have thus gained entrance increase in amount, and eventually
closely follow the upward growth of the stem during the whole

season. When this is about completed and the plant begins to develop its reproductive parts, the fungous threads become abundant just beneath the epidermis of the ovary and the stamens. This mass soon loses its identity as threads by the gelatinization of the cell walls and by the re-arrangement of cell contents. From this fertile stratum the spores are developed centripetally. Thus when the panicles appear we find their stamens and ovaries converted into seed-like bodies filled with a dusty mass of spores. These spores, if placed immediately in water, will germinate readily, a condition that also holds true for those that are a number of years old.

4. Experiments showed that the amount of smut ordinarily occurring in broom-corn can be greatly increased by mixing a liberal supply of smut with the seed before planting, but was not increased by planting seed in land that had smut in it or by placing smut on the plants after they appeared above ground.

5. These experiments show that the way to prevent smut is to use seed free from it or seed whose attached smut germs have been killed. This killing was accomplished by treating seed with hot water, 135° F., for ten to fifteen minutes. Ordinary seed that gave with check experiments from two to nearly twenty per cent. of smutted plants, when treated, gave plants free from the smut. Seed mixed with abundance of smut, when treated, produced plants while not always free from smut at least always with a much smaller per cent. of infected ones than similar seed not treated.

### PREVENTION OF BROOM-CORN SMUT

For the convenience of those who may wish to try the hot water treatment for the prevention of smut in their broom-corn, the following method of procedure is suggested. The station will be pleased to receive information as to the success of those who may try this, also any suggestions for improvement that use may bring out.

*Advisability.* From the experiments conducted it is seen that smut of broom-corn can be prevented or at least decidedly lessened in amount. It then becomes merely a question with each grower to decide whether or not the injury done to his crop during various years is sufficiently great to warrant the treatment. From the opinions heard expressed on this matter, it would seem that most broom-corn raisers think that methods favorable to the prevention of smut are desired. Beside the hot water treatment selection of seed free from smut is a means to the same end, and one that is generally recognized, although the reason is not always so clearly understood.   In either case it is to have the seeds free from living germs of the fungus when germination takes place, as that alone is the time when the smut germ can successfully infect the plant.   Selection of seed, however, unless one knows all about its history, is not safe, as by mere examination one can not tell whether or not it has spores present, unless it is rendered quite smutty.   Hot water treatment, on the other hand, is surer and involves no cost save the labor of treatment.   As the amount of broom-corn required to seed an acre is comparatively small the treatment is not nearly so tedious as is the quite similar operation with oats.

*Hot water method.*   The following is recommended as a method of treatment, mechanical details of which can be changed to suit the convenience of the operator.   A reliable thermometer and two vessels of hot water (one at a temperature of about 135° F., and the other at 135° F. with means for keeping it there either by fire, additional hot water or injection of steam) are needed for the operation.   The seed to be treated to the amount of a bushel or less is placed in a coarse bag which is immersed in the first vessel and then raised up and down until the seed has come to about the temperature of the water.   This should be quickly accomplished and is done so that the temperature of the second vessel will not be lowered when the bag is placed in it.   This is now done, and the temperature, as shown by the thermometer placed among the seeds, should be kept near 135° F.   If this temperature is allowed to go up any the seed is in danger of being injured, and if it goes down much the spores may not all be killed.   After being ten to fifteen minutes in the second vessel, the seed is removed and dried, when it is then ready for planting.   While it is not advisable ever to use very smutty seed, if such is used, most of the smutted kernels may be removed by immersion and stirring in water and then skimming off the floating ones.   A good many perfect seeds, however, are apt to be lost by this operation, as not all of the sound ones sink.   Hot water treatment should then be given the seed.

G. P. CLINTON, M. S.
*Assistant Botanist.*

## EXPLANATION OF ILLUSTRATIONS.

Plate I.   The upper engraving shows the brush from a plat of broom-corn whose seed was mixed with smut and then planted.   Over ten per cent. of the plants were infected.   The lower engraving shows the brush from a plat whose seed was mixed with smut and then treated with hot water at 140° for 15 minutes.   But one stalk of the 1321 stalks in this plat was infected.

Plate II.  Upper left hand engraving shows slightly enlarged smutted flowers of broom-corn.  Upper right hand engraving shows panicles of broom-corn ; the right one was free, and the other two were infected, the action of the fungus manifesting itself in the enlarged central axes.  The lower engraving shows at the right a free and at the left an infected panicle.

Plate III.  This shows details of spore infected parts of broom-corn.  Figs. 1–10 are magnified 4 or 5 diameters, figs. 11–13 about 10 diameters, fig. 14 about 250 diameters, figs. 15–16 about 500 diameters.

Figs. 1–9 show infected parts of flowers, a. stamens, b. pistil, c. scales.  In 1 mycelium was found; in 2 spores were beginning to be formed; in 3 stamens were free from mycelium and spore formation had just begun at apex of pistil ; in 4 stamens and pistil were both infected but free from each other ; in 5 the infected parts were blended together; in 6 stamens and pistil merely showed distinct at apex ; 7–8 show rare forms where all of the flower parts were infected ; 9 shows usual method of infection with glumes free ; 10 shows an ordinary uninfected seed enclosed in the glumes.  Figs. 11–13 show cross-sections through an infected body, a. false-membrane, b. mature spores, b[1]. immature spores, c. columella.  Fig. 11 represents section through apex, 12 through center, and 13 through base of the infected body which is composed of pistil and stamens.  Fig. 14 shows cross-section through base of a rather young infected body, a. representing false membrane composed of epidermal cells and sterile fungous threads, b. mature spores, b.[1] immature spores, c. columella.  Figs. 15–16 show more highly magnified sterile fungous cells (a.) and spores (b.), fig. 15 being drawn from smut on imported Chinese variety of sorghum, and 16 from broom-corn.

Plate IV.  This shows the mycelium of the smut in the tissues of broom-corn.  Fig. 1 magnified about 150 diameters, and Figs. 2–6 about 500 diameters.

Fig. 1 shows a cross-section through the epicotyl of germinating broom-corn, near union of epicotyl and leaf-sheath, a. representing mycelium, b. epidermis, c. parenchymatous cells of cortex, d. woody cells of central cylinder.  Fig. 2.  A more highly magnified part of 1.  This shows condition of mycelium about three weeks after spores were placed on seed.  Fig. 3.  Section through leaf near juncture of leaf-sheath and epicotyl, showing narrowing of mycelium in the epidermal cell where entrance was probably gained to the leaf.  The leaf-sheath had been removed and spores placed on base of the exposed young leaf.  Figs. 4–4[1].  Mycelium in pith cells of a mature plant, 4 from base of stalk and 4[1] from apex near panicle.  Fig. 5.  Mycelium in pith cells from top of stalk at time flowers are being formed.  Fig. 6.  Mycelium in pith cells 46 days after spores were placed on the seed.

Plate V.  This shows germination of spores of broom-corn smut, a. representing spores, b. pro-mycelium, b[1]. abstricted portions of pro-mycelium, c. sporidia and secondary sporidia, c.[1] germinating sporidia.  Magnified about 500 diameters.

Fig. 1.  Germination of spores in distilled water, 1 at end of 6 hours, 2 at end of 9 hours, and 3 at end of 24 hours.  Fig. 2.  Germination of spores in distilled water at end of 24 hours, showing origin of knee-joints and infection threads.  Fig. 3.  Germination of Kansas spores in distilled water.  Fig. 4.  Germination in distilled water of spores taken from inside of seed that had been soaked in hot water at 130° F. for 5 min.  These spores probably germinated in contact with air.  Fig. 5.  Germination at end of several days in a cell with only a film of water covering the spores.  Figs. 6–8.  Germination of spores in different fluids, 6 in distilled water, 7 in tomato-broth, 8 in beef-broth, this last showing only the condition of the sporidia.  Figs. 9–11.  Germination of spores in beef-broth, 9 at end of 19 hours, 10 at end of 22 hours, and 11 at end of 40 hours.

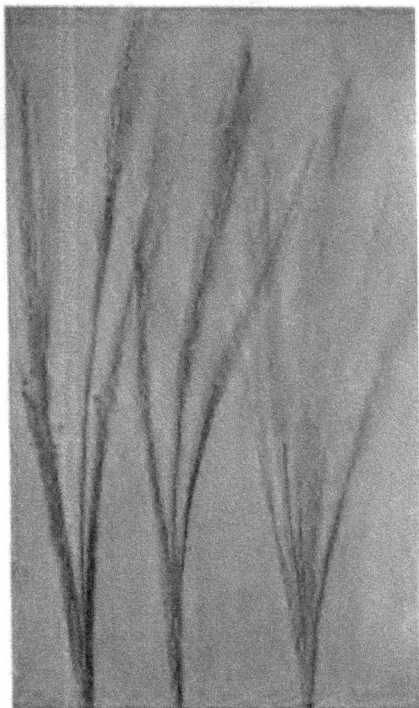

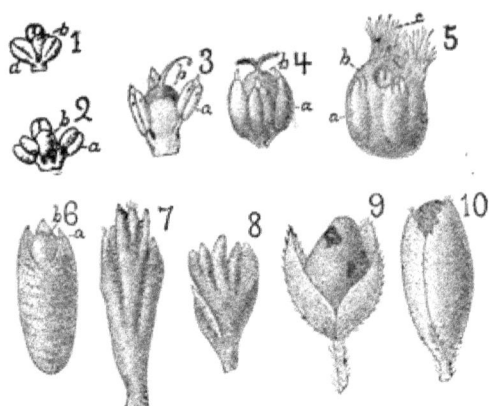
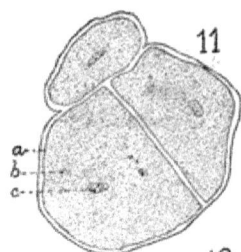
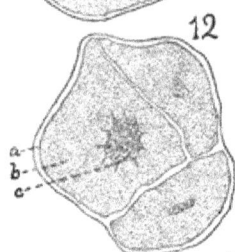
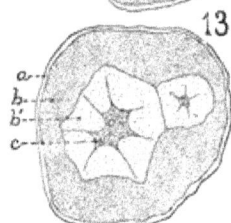
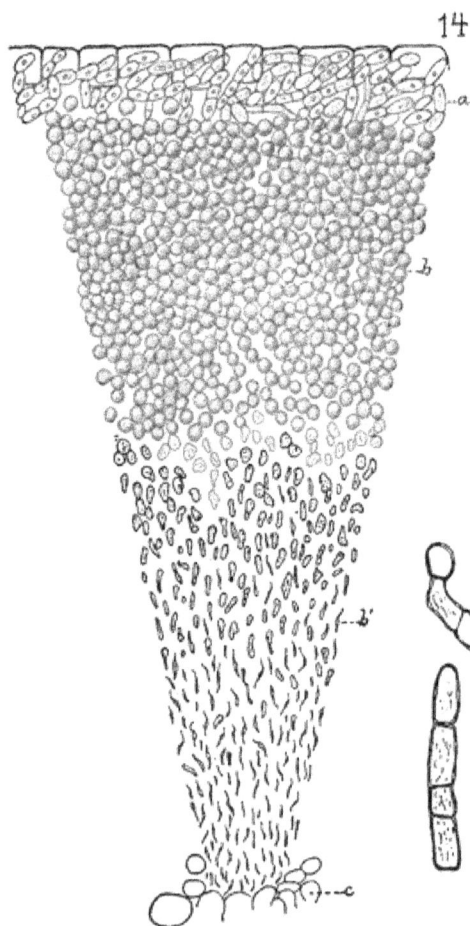
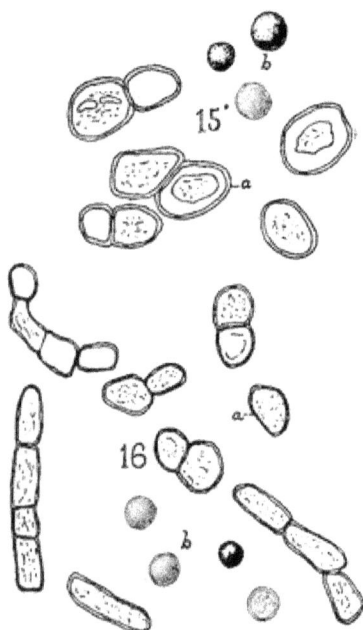

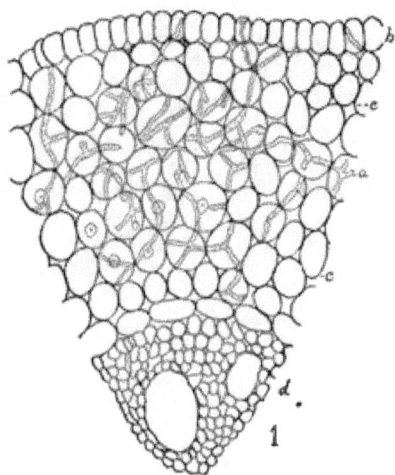

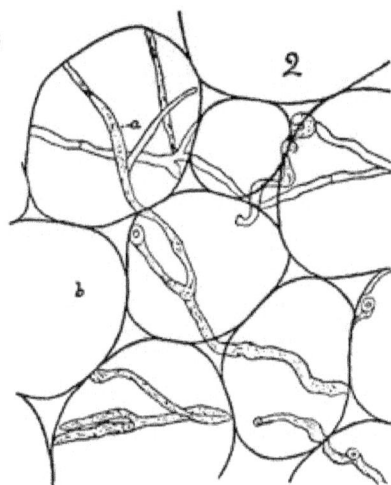

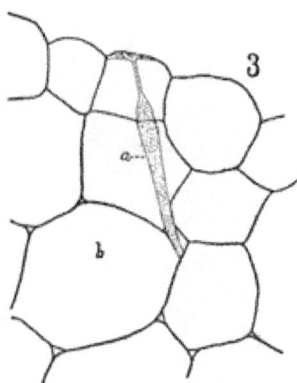

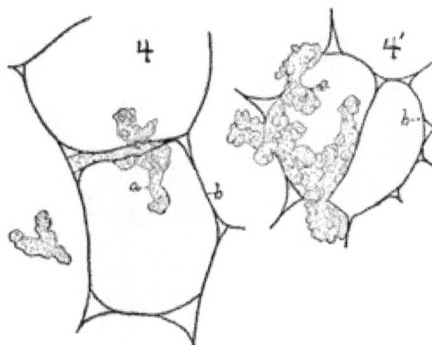

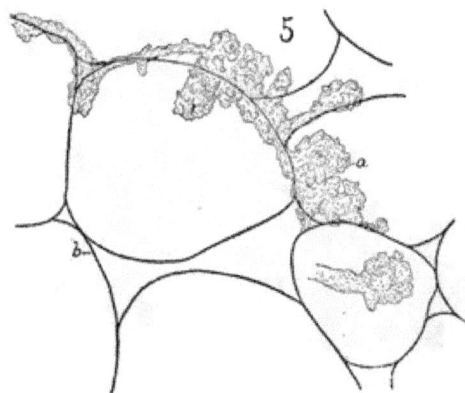

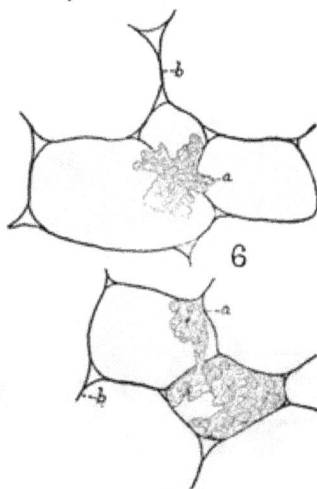

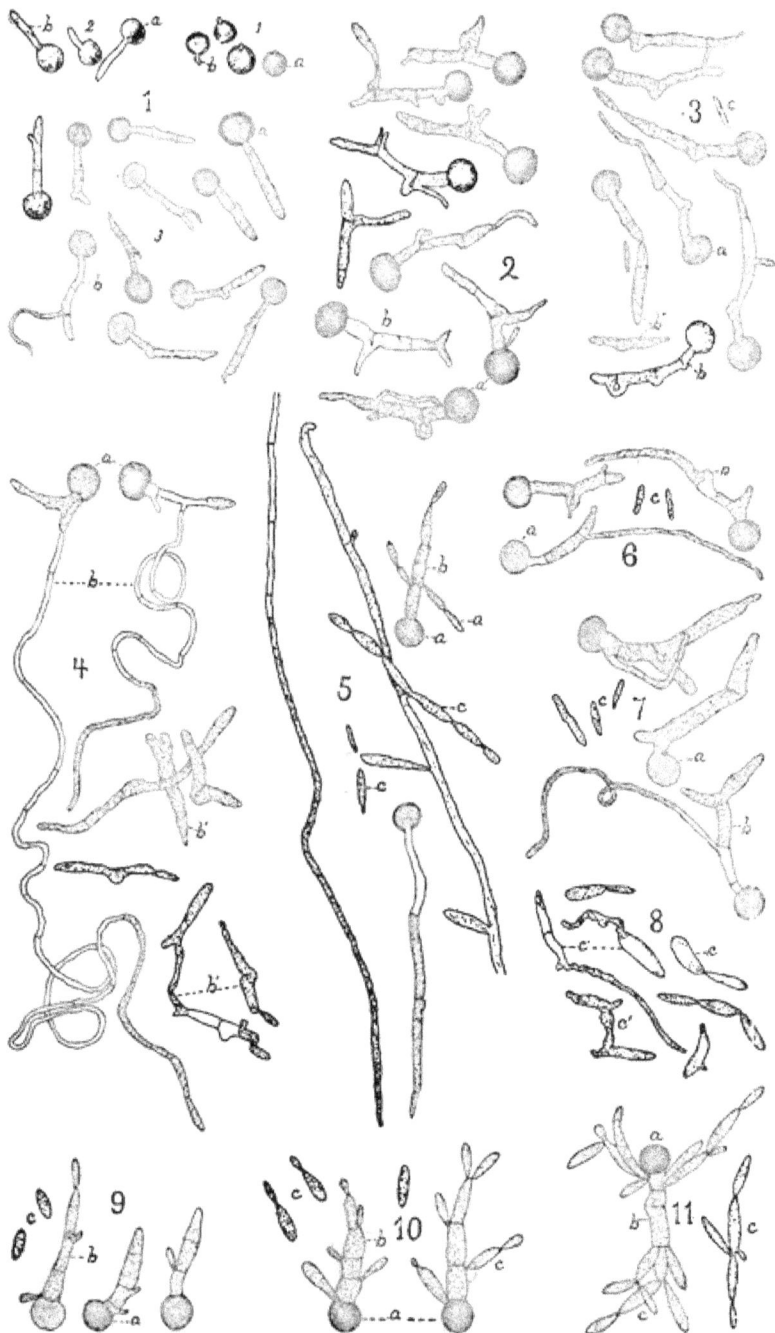